Easy Way To Find A Profitable Niche

The Ultimate Guide To Transform Your Perceived 'Inexperience' Into A Lucrative Asset

Mark J. Goines

Table of Contents

Author Bio:

Mark J. Goines is not only an author; he's a trailblazer in the realm of specialty entrepreneurship. With a passion for unearthing hidden potentials and transforming perceived inexperience into financial assets, Mark has become a guiding force for ambitious company visionaries.

Drawing on a plethora of experience in numerous industries, Mark is not your ordinary business guru; he's your friend in the pursuit of niche success. His path began with an obsessive curiosity for the untapped possibilities within niches, enabling him to develop tactics that surpass common wisdom.

Mark's innovative approach to entrepreneurship connects with individuals who dare to question the current quo. In "Easy Way To Find A Profitable Niche," he flawlessly integrates practical insights with motivating advice, providing a guide that not only informs but inspires.

Beyond the pages of his book, Mark is a compelling speaker and coach, sharing his insights on stages and platforms worldwide. His ability to demystify niche selection, validation, and monetization has garnered him honors as a thought leader in the entrepreneurial world.

Mark J. Goines is not only an advocate for niche success; he's a catalyst for revolution. Through his publications, speeches, and engagements, he continues to educate folks to use their apparent inexperience as a driving force for entrepreneurial prosperity.

So, if you're ready to start on a trip of discovery, guided by a seasoned entrepreneur who understands the intricacies of niche domination, Mark J. Goines is your trusted companion. Let his thoughts pave the route for your entrepreneurial victories, turning your perceived inexperience into the cornerstone of your specialty prosperity.

Introduction

Unlocking Your Niche Success

In the ever-expanding environment of entrepreneurship, establishing and cultivating your expertise is not simply a journey; it's a transformative process that may turn your perceived inexperience into a tremendous asset. This guide is your path to traverse the difficulties of niche investigation, validation, and monetization, guiding you from the beginning phases of niche discovery to the affluent heights of sustainable business growth.

For many ambitious entrepreneurs, the concept of creating a successful niche may seem like a daunting endeavor, especially when faced with the hurdles of apparent inexperience. However, this book is aimed to debunk the misconception that inexperience is a barrier to success. We'll highlight how your unique perspective and fresh approach may become the spark for identifying undiscovered prospects within a niche.

As we embark on this journey together, we'll delve into the principles of niche selection, explore effective tactics for validation, and equip you with the tools to monetize your passion successfully. Beyond that, we'll coach you on the path to gaining authority, and influence, and finally, scaling your specialty business for long-term prosperity.

Whether you're a seasoned entrepreneur looking to explore a new field or someone venturing into the world of business for the first time, this guide is geared to meet you where you are. Each chapter is a stepping stone, presenting actionable concepts, real-world examples, and case studies to clarify the path toward niche success.

So, if you're ready to change your perceived inexperience into a valuable advantage and go on a trip that promises not just earnings but a gratifying entrepreneurial enterprise, turn the page and let the exploration begin. Your successful niche awaits, and this book is your compass to navigate the path.

Chapter 1

Niche Finder

In the wide world of ideas, products, and services, identifying your specialty is analogous to unearthing a buried treasure chest. In the digital age, where opportunities abound, knowing the concept of a "niche" and learning how to discover one that suits your interests and expertise is vital for success. This chapter goes into the subtleties of niche finding, discussing what a niche is, why it matters, and how you might uncover the appropriate niche for your pursuits.

Defining the Niche

A niche is a specialized segment of the market for a certain kind of product or service. It's a distinct and specific area that caters to a unique audience with particular wants, tastes, or difficulties. Identifying a niche allows you to focus your efforts on a specified population, making your offers more relevant and desirable.

Why Niche Matters?

1. Competition: In a niche, you frequently encounter less competition compared to wide markets. This provides an opportunity to position yourself as an authority and cultivate a dedicated consumer base.

2. Better Understanding of Your Audience: When you cater to a certain niche, you can gain a deeper grasp of your audience's wants, issues, and desires. This understanding is crucial for producing products or services that resonate with your target market.

3. Increased Customer Loyalty: Niche audiences demand specialized attention. By addressing their wants, you may build a sense of loyalty among your clients, who are more likely to stick with a business that understands and responds to their specific demands.

How to Find Your Niche

1. Self-Reflection:
- Identify your passions, interests, and competence. What are you enthusiastic about?
  - Consider your talents and knowledge. What are you extremely good at?
  - Reflect on your experiences. Are there particular challenges you've encountered and addressed that others may be facing?

2. Market Research:
- Analyze current trends and market demands. What are people looking for?
  - Investigate your competition. Is there an underserved segment they might be overlooking?
  - Utilize tools and platforms like Google Trends, keyword research tools, and social media to uncover areas of interest.

3. Target Audience Analysis:
- Define your ideal customer. What are their demographics, behaviors, and preferences?
  - Consider pain spots and problems your audience confronts. How can you approach these concerns uniquely?

4. Evaluate Profitability:
- Assess the probable profitability of your chosen specialty. Is there a willingness to pay for items or services in this area?
  - Consider the scalability of your specialty. Can you extend and grow within it over time?

Case Studies

Explore real-world examples of individuals or enterprises that have effectively found and profited from their niche. Learn from their techniques, problems, and victories to obtain insights into how niche identification can lead to long-term success.

Finding your niche is not just about market positioning; it's about combining your passion with a specific audience's demands. In this chapter, we've created the groundwork for understanding the importance of niche markets, presented tactics for identifying them, and shared examples to inspire and guide you on your niche-finding quest.

As you engage in your exploration, keep in mind that the right niche is not just a lucrative market; it's a harmonious blend of your abilities, interests, and the needs of a certain audience.

Chapter 2

Is There A Good Niche?

In the search of selecting the proper niche, it's vital to delve into the concept of a "good" niche. Not all niches are made equal, and the quality of your chosen niche can substantially affect your performance. This chapter seeks to deconstruct the features of a good niche, helping you traverse the intricate world of alternatives and make informed judgments.

Defining a Good Niche

A good niche is more than just a section of the market; it's a place that coincides with your interests, offers development potential, and is well-suited to your abilities. To evaluate whether a niche is "good," numerous aspects need examination.

1. Passion and Expertise

An excellent specialization matches your hobbies and experience. When you're genuinely interested in and informed about a subject, your enthusiasm shines through in your work. This not only makes the experience more fun but also presents you as an authentic authority in your chosen sector.

2. Market Demand

While passion is vital, a good niche also meets market demand. Analyze whether there's a genuine need for items or services inside your chosen area. Are individuals actively seeking solutions or information about this area? Utilize market research tools and surveys to measure demand.

3. Competition Analysis

A good niche strikes a balance between being specific enough to decrease competition and wide enough to preserve profitability. Conduct a detailed competitive study to comprehend the landscape. A niche with too little rivalry could imply a lack of demand, while excessive competition can make it tough to stand out.

4. Target Audience Identification:

Understanding your target audience is crucial to niche success. A good niche helps you to accurately define your audience's features, preferences, and pain concerns. This knowledge enables you to personalize your services to match their demands, generating better ties and customer loyalty.

5. Profitability Potential

Consider the financial viability of your chosen niche. A solid specialty should give options for revenue. Assess whether your audience is willing to pay for items or services in this sector and analyze the possibility of scalability over time.

6. Trend Analysis

Trends play a key effect in niche viability. While evergreen niches have enduring appeal, it's equally vital to examine current trends. Be mindful of fads that may vanish fast, but also be open to developing trends that present potential for innovation and growth.

7. Personal Fulfillment

A successful niche should not only be financially profitable but also personally enjoyable. Success in an area you love can be more fulfilling than financial success alone. Consider whether your selected specialization matches your long-term goals and ideals.

Case Studies and Examples

Explore case studies of successful individuals or firms that have prospered in their chosen niches. Analyze how these examples match with the characteristics of a good niche, and extract significant lessons for your niche selection process.

The Ever-Changing Landscape

It's vital to know that the concept of a suitable niche is not static. Markets evolve, trends move, and customer preferences alter. Regularly examine your specialty to ensure it is aligned with your aims and continues to offer development opportunities.

In this chapter, we've discussed the multidimensional nature of a "good" niche. By examining elements such as passion, market demand, competition, and profitability, you can make informed decisions that build the foundation for long-term success. As you traverse the process of niche selection, remember that selecting a suitable niche is not only about joining a market but strategically placing yourself for sustained growth and fulfillment.

Chapter 3

50 Lucrative Sub-niches

Once you've grasped the necessity of establishing a good niche, the next step is to study the wide geography of sub-niches within that niche. Sub-niches offer a more detailed and specialized approach, allowing you to carve out a unique space in the market. In this chapter, we'll explore 50 lucrative sub-niches across several industries, presenting you with a varied choice of possibilities to consider for your entrepreneurial path.

1. Fitness and Wellness

1. High-Intensity Interval Training (HIIT) Workouts for Busy Professionals: Tailoring training routines for those with limited time.

2. Plant-Based Nutrition for Athletes: Addressing the nutritional demands of athletes using a plant-based diet.

3. Mindfulness Meditation for Stress Relief: A specialization centered on meditation approaches for stress management.

2. Technology and Gadgets

4. Smart Home Security Systems: Specializing in innovative home security solutions.

5. Virtual Reality (VR) Gaming Accessories: Catering to the expanding VR gaming community.

6. Eco-Friendly Tech Gadgets: Providing sustainable technology solutions.

3. Personal Finance

7. Cryptocurrency Investment Strategies: Navigating the intricacies of investing in digital currencies.

8. Financial Planning for Millennials:
Tailoring financial advice to the unique needs of the millennial generation.

9. Passive revenue Streams for Remote Workers: Exploring strategies to produce passive revenue while working remotely.

4. Travel and Adventure

10. Lone Female Travel Guides: Addressing the special issues and interests of lone female travelers.

11. Adventure Travel for Seniors: Providing adventurous travel alternatives tailored for senior citizens.

12. Sustainable Tourism Tips: Promoting eco-friendly and sustainable travel practices.

5. Home Improvement

13. DIY Smart Home Projects: Guiding homeowners in integrating smart home elements on their own.

14. Vertical Gardening Techniques: A specialty focused on space-efficient gardening solutions for urban inhabitants.

15. Upcycling and Repurposing Furniture: Transforming old furniture into fashionable and practical pieces.

6. Health and Nutrition

16. Keto-Friendly Dessert Recipes: Creating tasty treats for folks following a ketogenic diet.

17. Gut Health Optimization: Exploring approaches to improve gut health through nutrition and lifestyle.

18. Holistic Wellness for Busy Moms: Tailoring wellness practices for mothers juggling numerous commitments.

7. Business and Entrepreneurship

19. E-commerce Store Optimization: Helping online businesses maximize their sales and consumer engagement.

20. Dropshipping in Niche Markets: Exploring dropshipping prospects within certain niches.

21. Remote Team Developing Strategies: Assisting firms in developing cohesive remote teams.

8. Education and Learning

22. Coding for Kids: Introducing coding skills to youngsters through interesting instructional content.

23. Language Learning for tourists: Teaching practical language skills for tourists.

24. Personal Development for Introverts: Catering to the personal growth needs of introverted individuals.

9. Parenting and Family

25. Positive Discipline Techniques: A sub-niche focuses on positive and respectful parenting practices.

26. Single Parenting Resources: Providing assistance and resources for single parents.

27. Eco-responsible Parenting items: Showcasing sustainable and ecologically responsible parenting items.

10. Fashion and Beauty

28. Vegan Beauty Products Reviews: Evaluating and recommending cruelty-free and vegan beauty products.

29. Sustainable Fashion on a Budget: Curating economical and environmentally conscientious fashion alternatives.

30. DIY Natural Skincare Recipes: Crafting skincare products with natural and widely available materials.

11. Food and Cooking

31. Meal Prep for Weight Loss: Offering meal preparation help for people on a weight loss journey.

32. Gourmet Grilling Techniques: Elevating outdoor cooking using gourmet grilling ways.

33. Authentic Regional Cuisine Recipes: Exploring and sharing recipes from various places around the world.

12. Arts & Crafts:

34. Digital Illustration Tutorials for Beginners: Guiding prospective artists in the area of digital illustration.

35. Quirky Pet Portraits: Creating unique and whimsical portraits of people's pets.

36. DIY Wedding décor: Providing creative and budget-friendly wedding décor ideas.

This chapter has provided a broad array of 50 wealthy sub-niches, each giving distinct potential for research and specialization. As you review these possibilities, consider your passions, expertise, and the needs of your target audience. Remember, the secret to success lies not just in establishing a niche but in identifying a sub-niche that resonates strongly with your interests and allows you to deliver extraordinary value to your audience.

Use this list as inspiration, and feel free to mix and match parts to uncover a sub-niche that corresponds perfectly with your vision and ambitions.

Chapter 4

Validating Your Niche: Ensuring Profitability with Precision

Selecting a specialty is a key step in your entrepreneurial path, but the process doesn't end there. To achieve continued success, it's vital to validate your chosen specialty extensively. This chapter addresses the significance of niche validation and provides a complete guide on how to assure profitability with accuracy.

Understanding Niche Validation

Niche validation is the process of confirming that the niche you've identified has the potential to be profitable and sustainable. It comprises acquiring data, analyzing market dynamics, and determining the feasibility of your firm within the specified niche. Proper validation mitigates the risks associated with entering a market and raises the likelihood of success.

Key Steps in Niche Validation

1. Market Research and Analysis:

  - Demographics and Trends: Examine the demographics of your target audience and uncover any developing trends that could affect your specialty.

  - Competitor Analysis: Analyze your competitors to discover their strengths, weaknesses, and market positioning. Identify gaps or areas where you can differentiate yourself.

  - Keyword Research: Utilize tools like Google Keyword Planner to identify suitable keywords and measure search traffic. High search volume can indicate high interest in your niche.

2. Audience Feedback

  - Surveys & Questionnaires: Conduct surveys to obtain input directly from your target audience. Ask about their preferences, pain points, and the types of products or services they would be interested in.

- Social Media Engagement: Leverage social media tools to engage with your audience. Monitor discussions, comments, and reviews relating to your specialty to identify sentiment and acquire insights.

- Pilot Programs or Beta Testing:
Consider initiating a small-scale pilot program or beta testing to evaluate interest and gather input before a full-scale launch.

3. Monetization Potential

- Pricing Strategy: Assess the pricing sensitivity of your target audience. Experiment with different pricing strategies to achieve the ideal balance between profitability and customer happiness.

- Affiliate Marketing Opportunities: Explore prospective collaborations with affiliates to gauge interest in advertising your products or services within your expertise.

- Ad Revenue Potential: If content development is part of your strategy, examine the possibilities for ad revenue depending on the size and engagement of your target audience.

4. Prototype or MVP Testing:

- Minimum Viable Product (MVP): Develop a prototype or MVP to test the market. This helps you to evaluate your concept with real users and receive input for refinement.

- Iterative Improvement: Based on feedback from initial testing, iterate and improve your product or service to better suit the needs of your audience.

5. Long-Term Viability

- Scalability: Evaluate the scalability of your business inside the niche. Consider how you can develop and grow over time without compromising quality.

- Adaptability to Changes: Anticipate prospective changes in the market or industry and analyze how flexible your business is to these developments.

- Future Trends: Stay informed on upcoming trends that could affect your specialty, ensuring that your business remains relevant and inventive.

Case Studies in Niche Validation

Explore case studies of businesses that effectively verified their niches. Understand the tactics they employed, the obstacles they experienced, and how they adapted based on the feedback and data they got during the validation process.

Niche validation is a dynamic and continuing process that requires a combination of research, interaction, and flexibility. By taking the time to thoroughly validate your specialty, you position your organization for long-term success and prosperity. Remember that the insights discovered during validation can inform your marketing strategy, product development, and entire business approach. In the ever-evolving landscape of entrepreneurship, precision in niche validation is the key to developing a healthy and lasting firm.

Chapter 5

Monetizing Your Niche: Strategies for Sustainable Income

Successfully finding and validating your niche is a huge success, but the ultimate goal is to turn your passion and expertise into a sustainable income stream. This chapter discusses numerous ways to monetize your specialty efficiently, assuring not only profitability but also the life of your business.

Understanding Monetization in Your Niche

Monetizing your niche means translating the value you provide into revenue streams. It needs a smart approach that corresponds with your audience's preferences and your company model. Here, we'll cover a range of monetization tactics suited to diverse niches.

1. Product Sales

a. Physical Products:
 - E-commerce Store: Sell actual things relating to your niche through your e-commerce store. This could be items, specialist tools, or niche-specific commodities.

 - Print on Demand: Utilize print-on-demand services to develop and sell bespoke products without the need for inventory management.

b. Digital Products:
- E-books and Guides: Write and sell e-books or thorough guides addressing specific difficulties or delivering unique insights into your specialty.

 - Online Courses: Develop online courses or webinars to share your expertise with a paying audience.

 - Digital Art or Designs: If applicable, develop and sell digital art, designs, or templates.

2. Subscription Models

a. Membership Sites:
 - Exclusive Content: Offer premium, members-only content, such as in-depth articles, movies, or resources.

- Community Access: Create a secret group or forum where members may communicate, share insights, and access exclusive discussions.

b. Subscription Boxes:
- Curated Products: Curate and distribute subscription boxes featuring niche-specific merchandise.

- Instructional Materials: Include instructional materials or manuals about your niche in subscription box bundles.

3. Affiliate Marketing

- Product Recommendations: Partner with companies and promote their products or services, earning a reward for each sale made through your referral.

- Review and Comparison material: Create material reviewing and comparing products or services within your niche, integrating affiliate links.

4. Sponsored Content and Partnerships

- Collaborate with Brands: Work with brands relevant to your niche for sponsored content, where you display their products or services.

- Collaborations and Collaborations: Collaborate with other firms or influencers within your niche for joint ventures and mutually beneficial collaborations.

5. Advertising Revenue:

- Ad Placement: If your platform involves content development, try presenting adverts relevant to your niche to make advertising money.

- Podcast Sponsorships: If you broadcast a podcast, investigate sponsorships and partnerships with companies associated with your specialization.

6. Consultation and Services

- Freelancing: Offer your experience as a freelancer within your niche. This could involve writing, design, consultancy, or other services.

- One-on-One Coaching: Provide specialized coaching or consulting services to those seeking direction within your specialization.

7. Events and Workshops

- Hosting seminars or Seminars: Conduct in-person or virtual seminars and charge a participation fee.

- Event Sponsorships: Seek sponsorships for events or conferences relating to your niche.

8. Licensing and Syndication

- Licensing Your Content: License your content, such as images, videos, or written work, for use by other businesses or individuals.

- Syndication Agreements: Explore syndication agreements for your material to be presented on other platforms, reaching a bigger audience.

Case Studies on Monetization Success

Examine case studies of businesses or individuals within your niche that have successfully adopted monetization tactics. Analyze their tactics, obstacles experienced, and significant insights to influence your monetization plan.

Monetizing your niche is not a one-size-fits-all endeavor. It takes a smart and flexible approach that analyzes your audience, industry trends, and your unique value proposition. By diversifying your income streams and being responsive to your audience's requirements, you can establish a sustainable business that flourishes in the long run. Remember, the key to successful monetization comes in establishing a balance between profitability and giving actual value to your audience within your specialty.

Chapter 6

Niche Domination Blueprint: Building Authority and Influence

Having defined, validated, and monetized your niche, the next chapter in your entrepreneurial journey is to establish yourself as an authority inside your chosen domain. Niche domination goes beyond monetary achievement; it's about becoming a trusted voice, a go-to resource, and a respected personality. This chapter presents a detailed roadmap for gaining authority and influence in your area.

Understanding Niche Domination

Niche domination is the process of becoming the go-to expert and influential figure inside your niche. It entails not just exhibiting your knowledge but also generating a beneficial impact on your audience and industry. This authority not only increases your business's reputation but also offers other prospects for expansion.

1. In-Depth Knowledge

   - Continuous Learning: Stay abreast with the newest advancements, trends, and technology within your expertise. Regularly update your expertise to be a credible and informed authority.

   - Specialization: Consider specializing in a sub-niche or specific aspect of your field, allowing you to go deeper and establish unrivaled expertise.

2. Content Creation and Distribution:

   - High-Quality Content: Produce consistently high-quality content that educates, entertains, and engages your audience. This can be blog entries, videos, podcasts, or any medium that resonates with your target audience.

   - Multi-Channel Presence: Distribute your material across several channels, reaching a bigger audience and establishing your authority across diverse mediums.

3. Thought Leadership

- Opinion Pieces: Share your ideas and insights on industry trends, issues, and prospects. This places you as a thought leader inside your niche.

- Public Speaking: Participate in conferences, seminars, and podcasts as a guest speaker to offer your experience and increase your reach.

4. Engage with Your Community

- Active Participation: Engage with your audience on social media, forums, and other community platforms. Respond to comments, answer questions, and develop a sense of community around your expertise.

- Ask for Feedback: Encourage input from your audience and use it to develop your products. This not only develops trust but also shows your dedication to constant growth.

5. Networking and Collaboration

- Connect with Peers: Build relationships with other influencers, professionals, and businesses in your niche. Collaborate on projects, cross-promote content, and leverage each other's audiences.

- Interviews and Features: Seek opportunities to be interviewed by other influencers or media outlets within your niche.

6. Case Studies and Success Stories

- Showcase Results: Share case studies and success stories from your own experiences or those of your clients. Tangible achievements boost your authority and demonstrate the actual application of your expertise.

- Authentic recommendations generate trust and confidence.

7. Consistent Branding

- Brand Cohesiveness: Ensure that your brand identity is consistent across all platforms. This includes your logo, color schemes, message, and overall brand voice.

- This can include a professional website, a well-crafted bio, and a continuous presence on social media.

8. Continuous Innovation

- Adapt to Changes: Stay adaptive and receptive to innovation within your area. Embrace change, experiment with new ideas, and be at the forefront of developing trends.

- Launch New Initiatives: Introduce new projects, services, or products that demonstrate your commitment to innovation and advancement within your area.

Case Studies in Niche Domination

Explore case studies of individuals or firms that have successfully dominated their niches. Analyze their strategy, the milestones they reached, and how they maintained their authority over time.

Niche domination is a process, not a destination. By regularly showing your expertise, connecting with your audience, and responding to developments within your niche, you may establish yourself as a leading authority. Remember, authority is not only about what you know; it's about how you convey that knowledge and positively impact your audience. As you apply this template, stay committed to producing value, retaining authenticity, and growing with the ever-changing dynamics of your niche. In doing so, you'll not only dominate your area but also leave a lasting impact in your industry.

Chapter 7

Scaling Your Niche Business: From Profit to Prosperity

Scaling your niche business is the natural development after successfully finding, validating, monetizing, and developing authority within your niche. This chapter discusses the tactics and factors involved in taking your firm from a lucrative venture to a prosperous and sustainable enterprise.

Understanding Business Scaling

Scaling a firm entails growing its operations and influence to achieve sustainable growth. This can be achieved through many techniques, such as growing revenue streams, extending the client base, and streamlining internal procedures.

1. Diversification of Products and Services

 - New Offerings: Introduce complimentary items or services that correspond with your specialty. This not only responds to varied demands within your existing consumer base but also draws a broader audience.

 - Product Bundles and Packages: Create packaged offerings or packages that entice customers to purchase various products or services together, raising the average transaction value.

2. Geographic Expansion

 - Target New Markets: Identify and explore new geographical markets that share features with your present client base. Adapt your strategies to appeal to the distinct needs of these markets.

 - Global E-commerce: If applicable, consider expanding your e-commerce activities to reach a global audience. Ensure that your items or services can be easily accessible and shipped globally.

3. Strategic Partnerships and Collaborations

- Joint Ventures: Explore cooperative ventures with other businesses that complement your niche. These agreements can open new channels for growth and present your business to a wider audience.

- Cross-Promotions: Collaborate with other businesses or influencers for cross-promotions. This mutually beneficial method can greatly broaden your reach.

4. Automation and Technology Integration:

- Streamline Processes: Implement automation tools and technologies to streamline internal procedures. This not only boosts efficiency but also frees up resources for strategic growth efforts.

- Technology updates: Invest in technology updates that enhance the client experience and improve the scalability of your business.

5. Scalable Marketing Strategies

- Digital Marketing Channels: Optimize and grow your digital marketing activities. Explore new channels, optimize your targeting, and invest in techniques that have shown to be productive.

- Leverage their reach to introduce your brand to a bigger audience.

6. Customer Retention and Loyalty Programs

- Retention methods: Implement customer retention methods, such as loyalty programs, unique deals, and personalized communication. Retaining existing clients is often more cost-effective than obtaining new ones.

- Feedback Loops: Establish feedback loops to continuously improve your offers depending on customer input. Satisfied and engaged customers are more likely to become brand advocates.

7. Financial Management

- Profit Reinvestment: Reinvest a percentage of your profits back into the firm. This can include improving infrastructure, recruiting additional workers, or sponsoring new marketing campaigns.

- Financial Planning: Develop a robust financial plan that accounts for scaling efforts. Monitor key performance indicators (KPIs) and alter tactics as appropriate.

8. Employee Training and Development

- Skill Enhancement: Invest in training and developing your personnel to strengthen their skills. A well-trained team is more equipped to handle increased responsibilities and contribute to the company's growth.

- Developing a succession plan ensures continuity and stability during periods of growth.

Case Studies in Successful Scaling

Examine case studies of businesses that successfully scaled within your niche or a related industry. Analyze their growth strategies, challenges faced, and the key decisions that contributed to their prosperity.

Scaling your niche business is a dynamic and iterative process that requires strategic thinking, adaptability, and a commitment to continuous improvement. By diversifying offerings, expanding into new markets, and optimizing internal processes, you can propel your business from profitability to long-term prosperity.

Keep in mind that scaling is not just about increasing revenue; it's about creating a resilient and sustainable business that thrives in the face of evolving market dynamics. As you embark on this journey, maintain a balance between ambition and strategic planning, and be prepared to pivot when necessary. In doing so, you'll position your specialty firm for lasting success and profitability.

Conclusion

A New Horizon Awaits

As we complete our adventure through "Easy Way To Find A Profitable Niche: The Ultimate Guide To Transform Your Perceived 'Inexperience' Into A Lucrative Asset," take a minute to reflect on the transforming path you've walked. From the early quest to establish your specialty to the techniques adopted for validation, commercialization, and building authority, you've delved into the core of entrepreneurship.

This guide has been more than a compilation of strategies; it's been a companion, a mentor, and a source of inspiration. We've solved the riddle behind specialty selection, refuted the fallacies of inexperience, and celebrated the unique value you bring to the entrepreneurial table.

As you stand after this tutorial, remember that identifying a profitable niche is not a one-time event but an ongoing inquiry. The business landscape is changing, and your capacity to adapt and innovate will determine your continued success.

Now equipped with the tools to manage this dynamic landscape, you're set for the next chapter of your entrepreneurial career. Whether you're on the edge of beginning your niche business or currently navigating its early stages, take forward the lessons learned, the tactics identified, and the confidence gained.

Your perceived inexperience is no longer a constraint but a significant asset that allows you to identify chances others might overlook. Embrace the dynamic nature of entrepreneurship, constantly refining your specialization, and don't shy away from climbing new heights. Remember, the most successful entrepreneurs are those who regard obstacles as chances for growth.

As you turn the last page, see this not as an ending but as a prelude to the lucrative chapters that lie ahead. The world of specialized business is huge, and your journey is only just beginning. The profitable niche you've identified is not simply a market segment; it's an ecosystem where your passion, expertise, and uniqueness merge to produce something amazing.

So, take a deep breath, embrace the exciting unknown, and go confidently into the new horizon that awaits. Your entrepreneurial experience continues, and with the skills learned from this guide, you're well-equipped to develop your niche firm into a flourishing and enduring success.

May your journey be distinguished by ingenuity, resilience, and the steadfast belief that your perceived inexperience is, in fact, the very essence of your business prowess. Onward to wealth, and may your specialty venture illuminate the route to contentment and riches.